Be En

© 2010 by Barbour Publishing, Inc.

Written and compiled by Jennifer Hahn.

ISBN 978-1-60260-710-1

Published by Barbour Publishing, Inc., P.O. Box 719, Uhrichsville, Ohio 44683
www.barbourbooks.com

Our mission is to publish and distribute inspirational products offering exceptional value and biblical encouragement to the masses.

Member of the
Evangelical Christian
Publishers Association

Printed in China.

Be Encouraged

BARBOUR
PUBLISHING

I am thinking of you today, saying a prayer
that you might take heart, gather strength,
and be inspired to face your life with new energy.

Ellyn Sanna

Lord Jesus, I need encouragement today. Please bring someone into my path who can lift my spirits with life-giving words. Thank You for speaking through others so that my strength will be renewed. Amen.

The happiness of life is made up of minute fractions—
the little soon-forgotten charities of a kiss, a smile,
a kind look, a heartfelt compliment in the disguise of a
playful raillery, and the countless other infinitesimals
of pleasurable thought and genial feeling.

SAMUEL TAYLOR COLERIDGE

$\mathcal{O}$ Lord, You have heard the desire
of the humble; You will strengthen
their heart, You will incline Your ear.

PSALM 10:17 NASB

In a world where discouragement is prevalent, isn't it reassuring to know that God is bigger than any problem you face?

I will ask the Father, and he will give you another Helper to be with you forever.

JOHN 14:16 NCV

$\mathcal{D}$o not anticipate trouble, or worry about what may never happen. Keep in the sunlight.

BENJAMIN FRANKLIN

Have confidence in God's mercy,
for when you think He is a long way
from you, He is often quite near.

THOMAS À KEMPIS

When you must hurdle obstacles in your path,
if you can, observe the view from your
momentary higher vantage point.

$\mathcal{D}$o you ever wish you could live
"home on the range. . .where seldom
is heard a discouraging word"?
Make your life that kind of haven today.

$\mathcal{C}$haracter cannot be developed in ease and quiet. Only through experience of trial and suffering can the soul be strengthened, vision cleared, ambition inspired, and success achieved.

HELEN KELLER

*I*t is hard to fail, but it is worse
never to have tried to succeed.

THEODORE ROOSEVELT

Because God is the Master who stills storms,
He knows how to bring peace to a turbulent life.

$\mathcal{N}$ow may our Lord Jesus Christ Himself and God our Father, who has loved us and given us eternal comfort and good hope by grace, comfort and strengthen your hearts in every good work and word.

2 THESSALONIANS 2:16–17 NASB

*H*uman beings are created in the image of God,
able to both encourage and be encouraged.

There is no impossibility to him who stands prepared to conquer every hazard. The fearful are the failing.

SARAH J. HALE

So, my dear brothers and sisters, be strong and steady, always enthusiastic about the Lord's work, for you know that nothing you do for the Lord is ever useless.

1 CORINTHIANS 15:58 NLT

Next time you view yourself in a mirror,
view yourself as God sees you—
a special creation, made in His image.

There is no need to shoulder the weight of your cares any longer. God is right there, waiting for you to surrender your burdens to Him.

*O*ur greatest glory consist not in never falling, but in rising every time we fall.

OLIVER GOLDSMITH

We must not become tired of doing good.
We will receive our harvest of eternal life
at the right time if we do not give up.

GALATIANS 6:9 NCV

Don't worry about tomorrow.
God is already waiting there,
ready to help you through.

The supreme happiness of life is in the conviction
that we are loved; loved for ourselves,
or rather, in spite of ourselves.

VICTOR HUGO

Such things were written in the Scriptures long ago to teach us. They give us hope and encouragement as we wait patiently for God's promises.

ROMANS 15:4 NLT

The man who removes a mountain
begins by carrying away small stones.

CHINESE PROVERB

A burden, even a small one, when carried
alone and in isolation can destroy us,
but a burden when carried as part of God's
burden can lead us to new life. That is
the great mystery of our faith.

HENRI NOUWEN

The steadfast love of the Lord is from everlasting to everlasting, and you're right in the middle of His love.

When we go down the road of life and have made the wrong choice, remember that God will help us get back on the road going in the right direction.

Therefore if there is any encouragement in Christ, if there is any consolation of love, if there is any fellowship of the Spirit, if any affection and compassion, make my joy complete by being of the same mind, maintaining the same love, united in spirit, intent on one purpose.

PHILIPPIANS 2:1–2 NASB

It does not matter how slowly you
go so long as you do not stop.

CONFUCIUS

Remember that Jesus calls you "friend."

$\mathcal{W}$ake each morning with a sense of hope.
God has amazing things in store for you.
And He does all things well.

ELLYN SANNA

$\mathcal{W}$hat would life be if we had no courage to attempt anything?

VINCENT VAN GOGH

For momentary, light affliction is producing for us an eternal weight of glory far beyond all comparison.

2 CORINTHIANS 4:17 NASB

$\mathcal{D}$on't lose heart.
Jesus has you in His.

*K*eep your face upturned to [God]
as the flowers do the sun.
Look, and your soul shall live and grow.

HANNAH WHITALL SMITH

"The Lord's loved ones will lie down in safety,
because he protects them all day long.
The ones he loves rest with him."

DEUTERONOMY 33:12 NCV

God is our safe place where we can rest and be encouraged.

God has a path of life for us to walk. Though the path might be rocky at times, remember that He's always there, guiding each step, providing His presence.

$\mathcal{T}$here is nothing better than the encouragement of a good friend.

KATHARINE BUTLER HATHAWAY

When we take time to notice the simple things in life, we never lack for encouragement. We discover we are surrounded by limitless hope that's just wearing everyday clothes.

ANONYMOUS

*G*od's love for you is constant.
No matter how you feel,
He's there loving you.

Are you living with regrets? Do you find it hard to forget mistakes of the past? Jesus promises to forget sins when we confess them. In Isaiah 43:25, we are reminded, "I, even I, am the one who wipes out your transgressions for My own sake, And I will not remember your sins" (NASB).

$\mathcal{L}$ike apples of gold in settings of silver is a word spoken in right circumstances.

PROVERBS 25:11 NASB

The best way to cheer yourself is to
try to cheer someone else up.

MARK TWAIN

Have you met with Jesus today? He will encourage your heart as no one else can!

I can do all things through Christ,
because he gives me strength.

PHILIPPIANS 4:13 NCV

$\mathcal{D}$etermine that the thing can and shall be done, and then we shall find the way.

ABRAHAM LINCOLN

When you awoke this morning,
you were given a wonderful gift—
a brand-new day, a chance to "begin again."

$\mathcal{T}$hose whom we support hold us up in life.

MARIE VON EBNER-ESCHENBACH

May the Lord of peace himself always give you his peace no matter what happens.

2 THESSALONIANS 3:16 NLT

$\mathcal{W}$hen Jesus was on earth, He suffered temptations and trials just as we do. Ask Him for His help—He understands!

*I*magine every day to be the last of a life surrounded with hopes, cares, anger, and fear. The hours that come unexpectedly will be much the more grateful.

HORACE

The Lord's mercy often rides to the door of our heart upon the black horse of affliction.

CHARLES SPURGEON

$\mathcal{N}$obody trips over mountains. It is the small pebble that causes you to stumble. Pass all the pebbles in your path and you will find you have crossed the mountain.

AUTHOR UNKNOWN

Patience and encouragement. . .
come from God.

ROMANS 15:5 NCV

Are you feeling down? Take good care of yourself: eat well, exercise, and get a good night's rest. If you apply these practices, you will feel renewed in both mind and body.

Everyone needs to be encouraged—
you are no exception. Pastors, world
leaders, celebrities. . .no one is exempt.

$\mathcal{Y}$ou gain strength, courage, and confidence by every experience in which you really stop to look fear in the face. You are able to say to yourself, "I have lived through this horror. I can take the next thing that comes along.". . . You must do the thing you think you cannot do.

ELEANOR ROOSEVELT

$\mathcal{B}$ut, Lord, you are my shield,
my wonderful God who gives me courage.

PSALM 3:3 NCV

$\mathcal{D}$ear Father, I thank You for the many ways You have encouraged me. Just the fact that You know the number of hairs on my head shows that You declare me as valuable. Help me to remember to express my gratitude to You, and not to take Your love and care for granted. Amen.

It doesn't take a superhuman to be an encourager. In fact, words are often not even necessary. A smile or a hug can convey a heart full of support and love.

$\mathcal{L}$ife is not easy for any of us. But what of that?
We must have perseverance and above all confidence
in ourselves. We must believe that we are gifted for
something and that this thing must be attained.

MARIE CURIE

So humble yourselves under the mighty power of God, and in his good time he will honor you. Give all your worries and cares to God, for he cares about what happens to you.

1 PETER 5:6–7 NLT

Are you feeling as if everything is going wrong today? Take a moment to dwell on what is going right in your life. It may just give you that brief respite you need.

There are high spots in all of our lives and most of them have come about through encouragement from someone else.

GEORGE MATTHEW ADAMS

$\mathcal{P}$leasant words are like a honeycomb,
making people happy and healthy.

PROVERBS 16:24 NCV

*I*nstruction does much,
but encouragement does everything.

JOHANN WOLFGANG VON GOETHE

Sometimes we may feel as though we're in the pit of discouragement. At those times, we need to lift up our eyes, then reach up and put our hand in God's. He can pull us out of the pit and cause our hearts to sing.

Dear Lord, I pray that even though I feel as if I'm in an "encouragement deficit" that You will lead me to someone I can encourage. At times like those, we can even receive some encouragement just by helping someone else. Thank You for using me. Amen.

*B*ut you, brothers and sisters,
never become tired of doing good.

2 THESSALONIANS 3:13 NCV

In a world full of limits, it's hard to imagine something that is never ending. But God's love is limitless and unconditional— He will never stop loving you.

$\mathcal{W}$hen we do the best that we can,
we never know what miracle is wrought
in our life, or in the life of another.

HELEN KELLER

The LORD hears his people
when they call to him for help.
He rescues them from all their troubles.

PSALM 34:17 NLT

Are your worries keeping you awake?
Talk to God. He won't be sleeping or too busy.
He loves you and has time for you, as if you
were the only person in the world.

Thank God for those special encouragers
in your life. If you can't think of anyone,
pray that He will provide someone
to fill that need for you.

*W*hen you get to the end of your rope,
tie a knot and hang on.

FRANKLIN D. ROOSEVELT

In this you greatly rejoice, even though
now for a little while, if necessary,
you have been distressed by various trials,
so that the proof of your faith, being more
precious than gold which is perishable,
even though tested by fire, may be found to
result in praise and glory and honor at the
revelation of Jesus Christ.

1 PETER 1:6–7 NASB

Who would expect that Job would be an encourager? He himself suffered great loss: He lost his livestock, his children, and his health. Yet when his friends came to cheer him up—but didn't do a very good job—he said to them, "Instead, I would encourage you, and my words would bring you relief" (Job 16:5 NCV).

No matter how difficult, every step taken is one pace closer to the goal.

$\mathcal{A}$ word of encouragement during a failure is worth more than an hour of praise after success.

AUTHOR UNKNOWN

"*I* told you these things so that you can
have peace in me. In this world you
will have trouble, but be brave!
I have defeated the world."

JOHN 16:33 NCV

$\mathcal{D}$o you feel like the storms of life are rocking your boat? Think of the sailboat: The stronger the winds, the sooner it can find refuge in the harbor.

There is no failure except
in no longer trying.

ELBERT HUBBARD

God created you and has a purpose for your life. If the Creator of the universe fashioned you, you can know that you have infinite worth!

There is no God like you. You forgive those who are guilty of sin; you don't look at the sins of your people who are left alive. You will not stay angry forever, because you enjoy being kind. You will have mercy on us again; you will conquer our sins. You will throw away all our sins into the deepest part of the sea.

MICAH 7:18–19 NCV

$\mathcal{F}$latter me, and I may not believe you. Criticize me, and I may not like you. Ignore me, and I may not forgive you. Encourage me, and I may not forget you.

WILLIAM ARTHUR

Dear Father, someone gave me some constructive criticism today. Although I was a little hurt at first, I soon realized that they had my best interest at heart. Thank You for their boldness and compassion! Amen.

Everything we call a trial, a sorrow, or a duty,
believe me, that an angel's hand is there.

FRA GIOVANNI

The sun sets, plunging the earth into darkness; but it always rises again, spreading its rays and warmth over the world.

We who are still alive will be gathered up with them in the clouds to meet the Lord in the air. And we will be with the Lord forever.

1 THESSALONIANS 4:17 NCV

When you get in a tight place and everything goes against you, until it seems as if you could not hold on a minute longer, never give up then, for that is just the place and time when the tide will turn.

HARRIET BEECHER STOWE

*H*e takes care of his people like a shepherd.
He gathers them like lambs in his arms
and carries them close to him.

Isaiah 40:11 NCV

It takes time for a caterpillar to turn into a butterfly, and for a tadpole to turn into a frog. That span of time is necessary for the miracle of transformation that occurs. When the marvelous creation is finally beheld, those moments of waiting fade from memory.

Thank You, Lord, for the gift of friends You have given me. Bless those who encourage me, and give me the compassion to encourage others. Amen.

All progress occurs because people dare to be different.

HARRY MILLNER

For the LORD grants wisdom! From his mouth come knowledge and understanding. He grants a treasure of good sense to the godly. He is their shield, protecting those who walk with integrity. He guards the paths of justice and protects those who are faithful to him.

PROVERBS 2:6–8 NLT

When you come to the end of all the light
you know, and it's time to step into the
darkness of the unknown, faith is knowing
that one of two things shall happen: Either
you will be given something solid to stand
on or you will be taught to fly.

EDWARD TELLER

$\mathcal{D}$ear Jesus, thank You for that one who listens to me with open ears and heart, but also lifts me up with kind words. What a blessing! Amen.

$\mathcal{Y}$ou may be disappointed if you fail,
but you are doomed if you don't try.

BEVERLY SILLS

You can be sure that the more we suffer for Christ, the more God will shower us with his comfort through Christ.

2 CORINTHIANS 1:5 NLT

So, amid the conflict
whether great or small,
Do not be disheartened, God is over all;
Count your many blessings,
angels will attend,
Help and comfort give you to
your journey's end.

JOHNSON OATMAN, JR.

In Acts 4:36, Barnabas is called the "Son of Encouragement." He may have been named so because of verbal encouragement he offered, but he was supportive in his actions as well. In verse 37, we are told that he sold a piece of land and gave all the proceeds to the apostles. What a humble and selfless act of encouragement!

The sufferings we have now are
nothing compared to the great
glory that will be shown to us.

ROMANS 8:18 NCV

Every calling is great when greatly pursued.

OLIVER WENDELL HOLMES

*D*ear Jesus, I sometimes feel as if I'm constantly being beaten up—maybe not physically, but mentally and emotionally. Although I appreciate encouragement from others, help me not to depend on them. May I look to You as my constant and true source of encouragement. Amen.

The LORD will always lead you. He will satisfy your needs in dry lands and give strength to your bones. You will be like a garden that has much water, like a spring that never runs dry.

ISAIAH 58:11 NCV

I believe that any man's life will be filled with constant and unexpected encouragement, if he makes up his mind to do his level best each day, and as nearly as possible reaching the high water mark of pure and useful living.

BOOKER T. WASHINGTON

*I*f we had no winter, the spring would not be so pleasant; if we did not sometimes taste adversity, prosperity would not be so welcome.

ANNE BRADSTREET

*C*orrection does much, but encouragement does more. Encouragement after censure is as the sun after a shower.

JOHANN WOLFGANG VON GOETHE

Bless the LORD, O my soul, and forget none of His benefits; who pardons all your iniquities, who heals all your diseases; who redeems your life from the pit, who crowns you with lovingkindness and compassion; who satisfies your years with good things, so that your youth is renewed like the eagle.

PSALM 103:2–5 NASB

$\mathcal{D}$ear Father, sometimes I don't feel worthy of encouragement. At those times, I need Your help to see myself as You see me— a unique person, created in Your image. Amen.

We need never shout across the spaces to an absent God. He is nearer than our own soul, closer than our most secret thoughts.

A. W. TOZER

All Scripture is inspired by God and is
useful to teach us what is true and to make
us realize what is wrong in our lives.
It straightens us out and teaches us to
do what is right.

2 TIMOTHY 3:16 NLT

*I*t is not enough to help the feeble up,
but to support him after.

WILLIAM SHAKESPEARE

God came to us because God wanted to join us on the road, to listen to our story, and to help us realize that we are not walking in circles but moving toward the house of peace and joy.

THOMAS MERTON

I am still determined to be cheerful and happy, in whatever situation I may be; for I have also learned from experience that the greater part of our happiness or misery depends upon our dispositions, and not upon our circumstances.

MARTHA WASHINGTON

I call to you in times of trouble,
because you will answer me.

PSALM 86:7 NCV

What are some qualities of an encourager? Would you describe that person as motivated, humble, positive? There are many other traits that could be added to that list. If we choose a couple to hone in our own lives, we will be more able to encourage others in the way that they encouraged us.

The Lord is my rock, my protection, my Savior. My God is my rock. I can run to him for safety. He is my shield and my saving strength, my defender. I will call to the LORD, who is worthy of praise, and I will be saved from my enemies.

PSALM 18:2–3 NCV

$\mathcal{T}$ry not to become a man of success
but a man of value.

ALBERT EINSTEIN

$\mathcal{W}$hen it is dark enough,
you can see the stars.

CHARLES BEARD

$\mathcal{W}$ithout sweat and toil no work is made perfect.

LATIN PROVERB

So when we are weighed down with troubles, it is for your benefit and salvation! For when God comforts us, it is so that we, in turn, can be an encouragement to you. Then you can patiently endure the same things we suffer.

2 Corinthians 1:6 nlt

*I*f doing a good act in public will excite others
to do more good, then. . ."Let your shine to all. . ."
Miss no opportunity to do good.

JOHN WESLEY

When you face discouragement,
take a look at your fingerprint. No one else
has the same one—you are one of a kind.
The God who fashioned that fingerprint
holds you in His hand.

$\mathcal{W}$e learn wisdom from failure much more than success. We often discover what we will do, by finding out what we will not do.

SAMUEL SMILES

$\mathcal{W}$orry is a heavy load,
but a kind word cheers you up.

PROVERBS 12:25 NCV

Can you think of someone who has encouraged you? Why not give them a call, write a note, or send an e-mail thanking them for the words or actions that lifted your spirits. In expressing your thanks, you will be an encouragement to them.

The world is in dire need of encouragers.

G. E. DEAN

I think these difficult times have helped me to understand better than before how infinitely rich and beautiful life is in every way and that so many things that one goes around worrying about are of no importance whatsoever.

ISAK DINESEN

$\mathcal{T}$he talent of success is nothing more than doing what you can do, well.

HENRY W. LONGFELLOW

$\mathcal{D}$raw close to God, and God will draw close to you.

JAMES 4:8 NLT

*I*f you find you are constantly discouraged in certain situations or surroundings, you may need to remove those sources of discouragement. Ask the Lord to direct your paths so that you can find a more encouraging environment.

My help comes from the LORD, who made heaven and earth. He will not allow your foot to slip; He who keeps you will not slumber.

PSALM 121:2–3 NASB

*I*f you do not hope, you will not find what is beyond your hopes.

ST. CLEMENT OF ALEXANDRIA

Jesus is the Light of the World. . .the lighthouse that draws us toward the hope of heaven.

HOLLEY ARMSTRONG

Dear Lord, I thank You for Your Word. Thank You for the encouragement it brings to me when I feel discouraged. Please speak to me as I read the scriptures. Amen.

$\mathcal{Y}$ou cannot plough a field by
turning it over in your mind.

AUTHOR UNKNOWN

So be strong and take courage,
all you who put your hope in the LORD!

PSALM 31:24 NLT

$\mathcal{L}$et us be of good cheer, remembering
that the misfortunes hardest to bear
are those that never happen.

JAMES RUSSELL LOWELL

Encouragement may be individual, but it could also be communal. In Acts 9:31 (NCV), we are told, "Respecting the Lord by the way they lived, and being encouraged by the Holy Spirit, the group of believers continued to grow." Pray for the encouragement of your church today.

It is only when the sea is moonless
that the Lord becomes my Light.

Elisabeth Eliot

An infinite God can give all of Himself to each of His children. He does not distribute Himself that each may have a part, but to each one He gives all of Himself as fully as if there were no others.

A. W. TOZER

*I*f you would know the road ahead,
ask someone who has traveled it.

CHINESE PROVERB

He will destroy death forever.
The Lord GOD will wipe away
every tear from every face.

ISAIAH 25:8 NCV

When everything seems to be going against you,
remember that the airplane takes off
against the wind, not with it.

HENRY FORD

Have you never heard or understood?
Don't you know that the LORD is the
everlasting God, the Creator of all the
earth? He never grows faint or weary.
No one can measure the depths of his
understanding. He gives power to those
who are tired and worn out; he offers
strength to the weak.

ISAIAH 40:28–29 NLT

$\mathcal{T}$hose who are lifting the world upward and onward
are those who encourage more than criticize.

ELIZABETH HARRISON

The Word of God is. . .
an infallible guiding light for hearts.

Owen Ford Faulkenberry

You are here to enrich the world.

WOODROW WILSON

In Philippians 1:14, Paul notes that because of his imprisonment, others were encouraged to speak the Word of God. Although he would have preferred to not have been incarcerated, God used that tribulation to spread the Good News further. What may look like a trial may just encourage others in their walk with God.

$\mathcal{M}$ost of us, swimming against the tides of trouble the world knows nothing about, need only a bit of praise or encouragement—and we will make the goal.

JEROME P. FLEISHMAN

$\mathcal{C}$ome, let us worship and bow down. Let us kneel before the LORD our maker, for he is our God. We are the people he watches over, the sheep under his care. Oh, that you would listen to his voice today!

PSALM 95:6–7 NLT

The finest gift you can give anyone is encouragement. Yet, almost no one gets the encouragement they need to grow to their full potential. If everyone received the encouragement they need to grow, the genius in most everyone would blossom and the world would produce abundance beyond our wildest dreams.

SIDNEY MADWED

We encouraged you, we urged you, and we insisted that you live good lives for God, who calls you to his glorious kingdom.

1 THESSALONIANS 2:12 NCV

The probability that we may fail in the struggle ought not to deter us from the support of a cause we believe to be just.

ABRAHAM LINCOLN

Yet those who wait for the LORD will gain new strength; they will mount up with wings like eagles, they will run and not get tired, they will walk and not become weary.

ISAIAH 40:31 NASB

I think and think for months and years,
ninety-nine times, the conclusion is false.
The hundredth time I am right.

ALBERT EINSTEIN

Dear Father, thank You for Your free gift of forgiveness. When I feel unforgivable, help me to remember that You have promised to remove my sins "as far as the east is from the west" (Psalm 103:12 NASB). You love me and have paid the penalty for my sins. I praise You! Amen.

$\mathcal{N}$ow, God be prais'd, that to believing souls
Gives light in darkness, comfort in despair!

SHAKESPEARE

If you would attain to what you are not yet, you must always be displeased by what you are. For where you are pleased with yourself there you have remained. Keep adding, keep walking, keep advancing.

Saint Augustine of Hippo

The Twenty-third Psalm speaks of walking "through the valley of the shadow of death" (verse 4 NASB). This chapter is most often read in times of grief and loss, but we need to remember that it speaks of walking *through* the valley, not *to the end* of the valley. God will be there to comfort us as we walk *through* the valley, until we safely emerge on the other side.

Some people come into our lives,
leave footprints on our hearts,
and we are never the same.

AUTHOR UNKNOWN

*G*od's ways seem dark, but soon or late,
they touch the shining hills of day.

Keep your face to the sunshine
and you cannot see the shadow.

HELEN KELLER

"*C*ome to Me, all who are weary and heavy-laden, and I will give you rest."

MATTHEW 11:28 NASB

*K*ind words can be short and easy to speak,
but their echoes are truly endless.

MOTHER TERESA

$\mathcal{W}$e all have different gifts, each of which came because of the grace God gave us. . . . Whoever has the gift of encouraging others should encourage.

ROMANS 12:6, 8 NCV

*N*ever give up, for that is just the place
and time that the tide will turn.

HARRIET BEECHER STOWE

Of all the forces that make for a better world,
none is so indispensable, none so powerful, as hope.

CHARLES SAWYER

$\mathcal{W}$hat men and women need is
encouragement. . . . Instead of always
harping on a man's faults, tell him
of his virtues. Try to pull him out
of his rut of bad habits.

ELEANOR H. PORTER

*I*f we endure hardship, we will reign with him.

2 TIMOTHY 2:12 NLT

$\mathcal{N}$ote how good you feel after you have encouraged someone else. No other argument is necessary to suggest that never miss the opportunity to give encouragement.

GEORGE M. ADAMS

$\mathcal{D}$ear Father, please help me to remember that You may choose to use trials in my life to encourage others. Help me to be patient in that process, so that they may receive Your gift of encouragement through my empathy. Amen.

"He will remove all of their sorrows, and there will be no more death or sorrow or crying or pain. For the old world and its evils are gone forever."

REVELATION 21:4 NLT

What an encouragement to know that for all believers, this world is not our home forever. We will be united with our precious Lord and all of His followers throughout eternity, enjoying the blessings that He has prepared for us.

Success is the sum of small efforts,
repeated day in and day out.

ROBERT COLLIER

And after you suffer for a short time, God,
who gives all grace, will make everything right.
He will make you strong and support you and keep
you from falling. He called you to share in his glory
in Christ, a glory that will continue forever.

1 PETER 5:10 NCV

$\mathcal{L}$et no one ever come to you without leaving better and happier. Be the living expression of God's kindness: kindness in your face, kindness in your eyes, kindness in your smile.

MOTHER TERESA

Do you know one of the greatest cheerleaders of all time? Paul, of the New Testament. Despite trials, he constantly found ways to build others up. In 2 Corinthians 7:4 (NCV), he wrote, "I feel very sure of you and am very proud of you. You give me much comfort, and in all of our troubles I have great joy."

Dear Lord, I pray that I can be a cheerleader for others as Paul was. Help me to look beyond my difficulties, so that I can root for others. Amen.

"They are blessed who grieve,
for God will comfort them."

MATTHEW 5:4 NCV

$\mathcal{W}$hatever you are, be a good one.

ABRAHAM LINCOLN

Sing for joy, O heavens! Rejoice, O earth!
Burst into song, O mountains! For the LORD
has comforted his people and will have
compassion on them in their sorrow.

ISAIAH 49:13 NLT

May the road rise to meet you. May the wind always be at your back. May the sun shine warm upon your face, the rains fall soft upon your fields and, until we meet again, may God hold you in the palm of his hand.

IRISH BLESSING

"*Be* sure of this: I am with you always,
even to the end of the age."

MATTHEW 28:20 NLT